SWIFT

COLORING BOOK

www.PlumStreetPressBooks.com

NORTH AMERICA
ATLANTIC OCEAN
PACIFIC OCEAN
SOUTH AMERICA
ATLANTIC OCEAN
WOW! AMAZING!

ARCTIC OCEAN
EUROPE
ASIA
AFRICA
PACIFIC OCEAN
INDIAN OCEAN
AUSTRALIA
SOUTHERN OCEAN
ANTARCTICA

SOUTH AMERICA

NORTH AMERICA

GREENLAND
CANADA

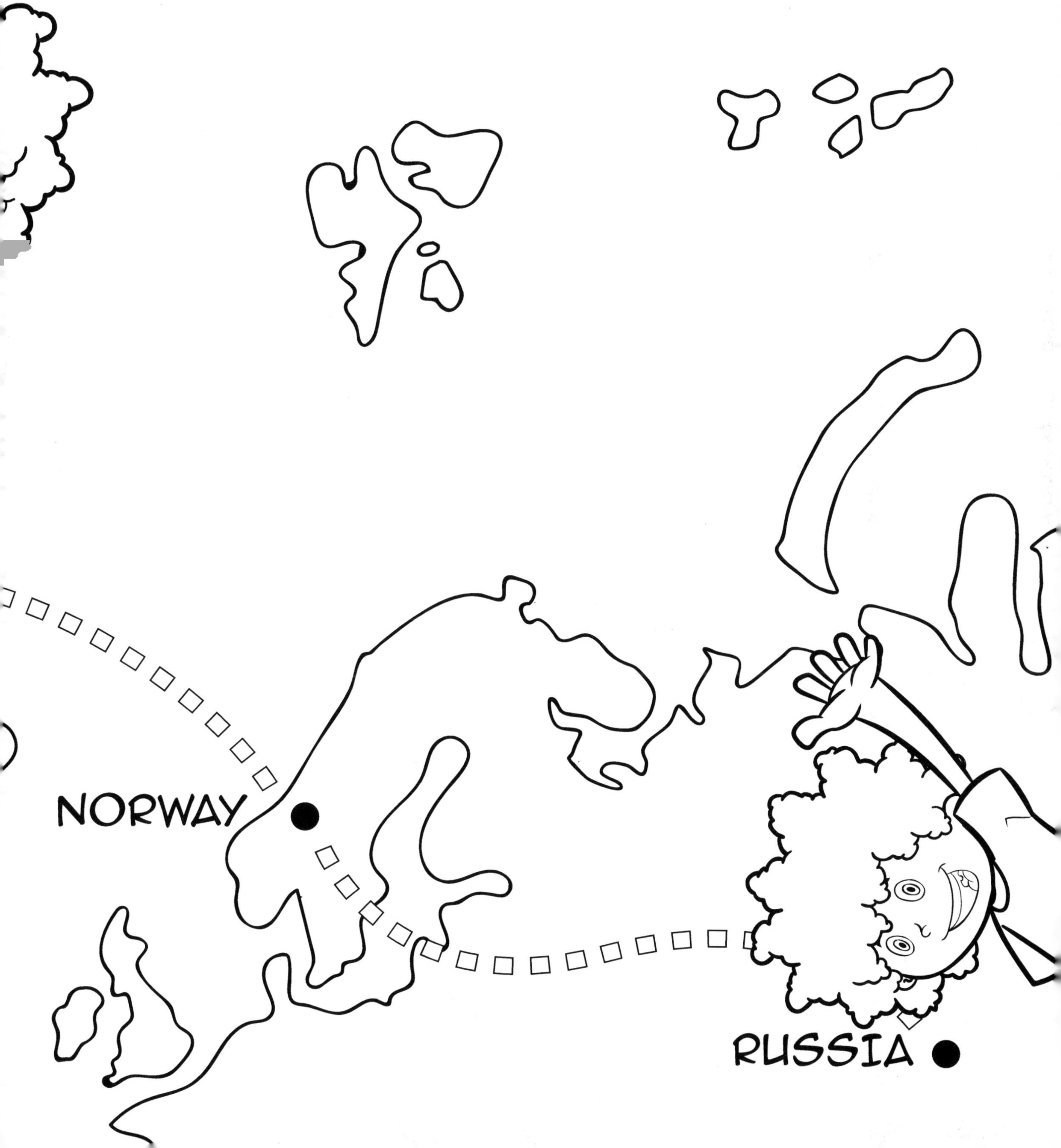
NORWAY
RUSSIA

EUROPE

AS

A

AUS

STRALIA

ANTAR

CTICA

AFRICA

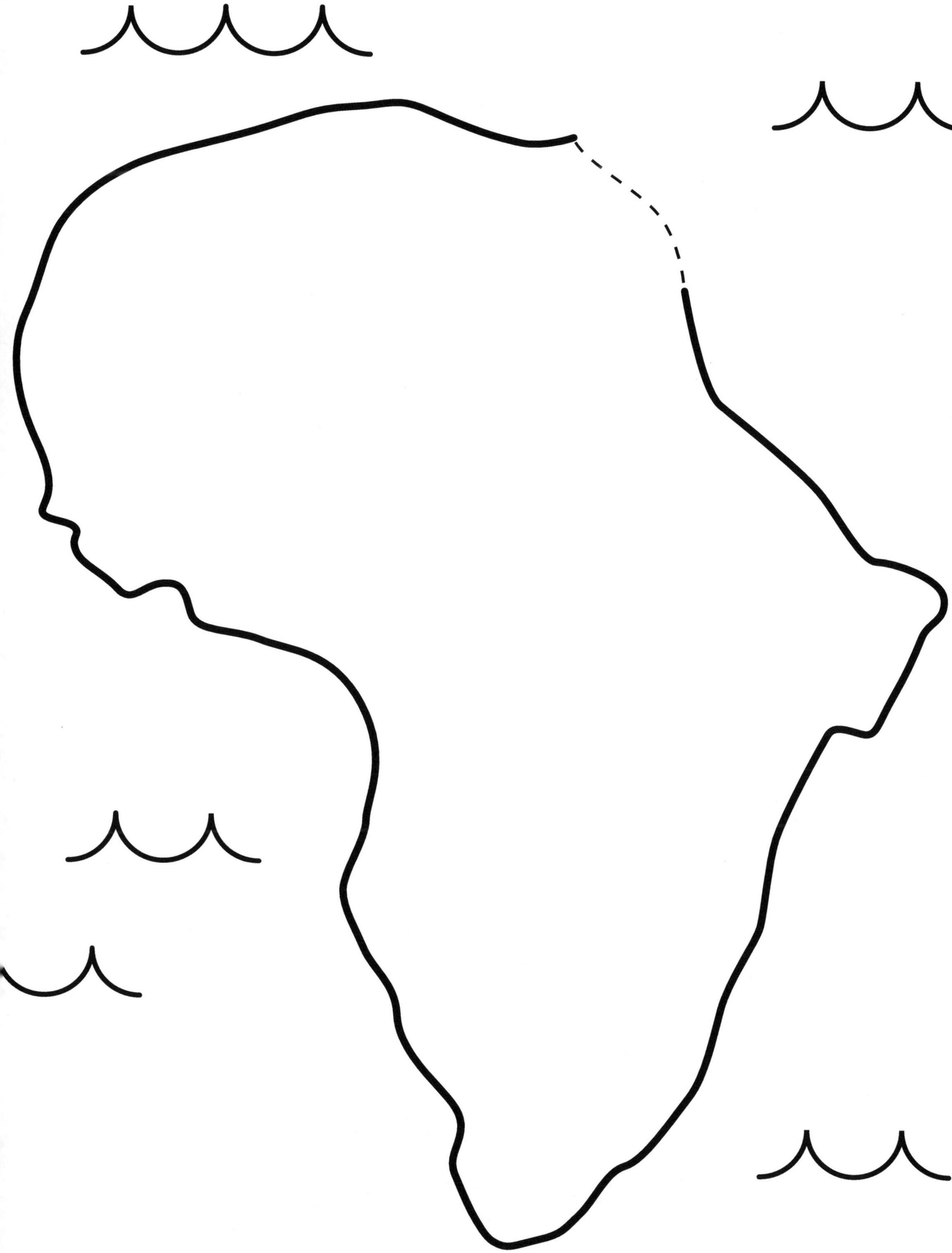

AUKE BAY
POTOMAC RIVER
HORSEHOE BEND
MOUNT COTOPAXI
AMAZON RAINFOREST
ATACAMA DESERT

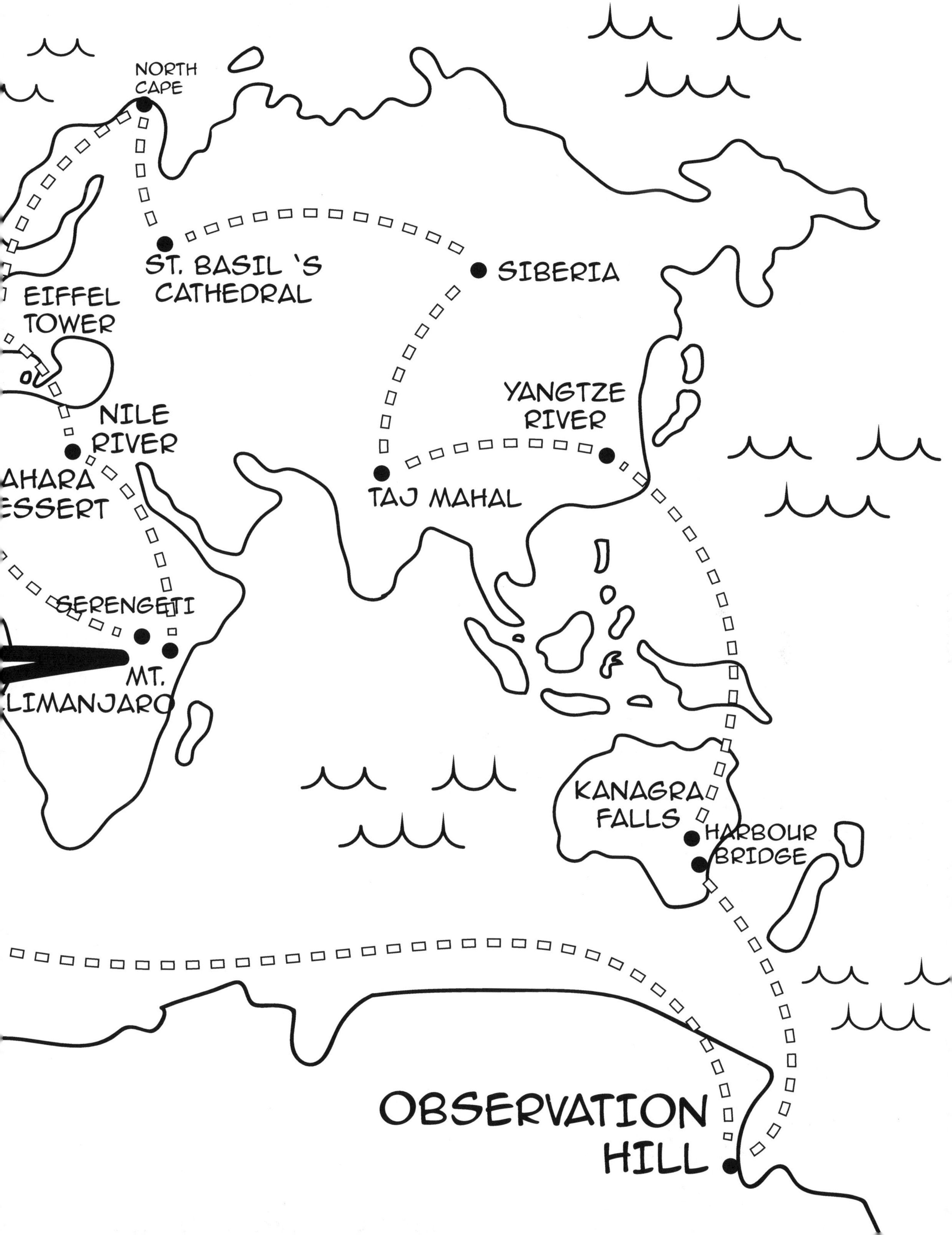
NORTH CAPE
ST. BASIL 'S CATHEDRAL
SIBERIA
EIFFEL TOWER
NILE RIVER
AHARA ESSERT
YANGTZE RIVER
TAJ MAHAL
SERENGETI
MT. LIMANJARO
KANAGRA FALLS
HARBOUR BRIDGE
OBSERVATION HILL

49149456R00030

Made in the USA
Middletown, DE
07 October 2017